JOHN JUERN

NORTHWESTERN PUBLISHING HOUSE
MILWAUKEE, WISCONSIN

Cover photos: Designpics, ShutterStock, Inc., SuperStock, Inc.
Art Director: Karen Knutson
Designer: Pamela Dunn

Scripture is taken from the HOLY BIBLE, NEW INTERNATIONAL VERSION®. NIV®. Copyright © 1973, 1978, 1984 by International Bible Society. Used by permission of Zondervan. All rights reserved.

The "NIV" and "New International Version" trademarks are registered in the United States Patent and Trademark Office by International Bible Society. Use of either trademark requires the permission of International Bible Society.

All rights reserved. No part of this publication may be reproduced, stored in a retrieval system, or transmitted in any form or by any means—electronic, mechanical, photocopying, recording, or otherwise—except for brief quotations in reviews, without prior permission from the publisher.

Second printing, 2007

Library of Congress Control Number: 2005922840
Northwestern Publishing House
1250 N. 113th St., Milwaukee, WI 53226-3284
www.nph.net
© 2006 by Northwestern Publishing House
Published 2006
Printed in the United States of America
ISBN: 978-0-8100-1304-9

To my children,

my grandchildren,

and all the children with whom

I've been privileged to work.

Contents

	Foreword vii
1	Obedience and the Heart 1
2	Responsibility and Kids 3
3	Trust and the Parent-Child Relationship 5
4	Spanking 7
5	Honesty 9
6	Compulsive Lying 11
7	The Twos 13
8	The Fantasy World of Children 15
9	Treating Attention Deficit/ Hyperactivity Disorder 17
10	Teaching Problem Solving 19
11	When Parents Are Afraid to Parent 21
12	Time-Outs 23
13	Do Your Children Know You Love Them? 25
14	Order in the Family 27
15	Attitudes about School 29
16	Crime and Consequence 31
17	Learning and the Senses 33
18	Neuroscience 35
19	Drugs and Alcohol 37
20	Childhood Depression 39

21	Suicide	41
22	At Times of Loss	43
23	Beyond Stress	45
24	Potty Training	47
25	Bed-Wetting	49
26	Spiritual Strength	51
27	Stuttering	53
28	Negative Attitude	55
29	Narcissism	57
30	Birth Order	59
31	Christian Discipline Is	61
32	Separation Anxiety	63
33	Memorizing Scripture	65
34	Compliant and Defiant Siblings	67
35	When Learning Becomes a Struggle	69
36	Homework Headaches	71
37	Repeating a Grade	74
38	When Parents Argue	77
39	Stop Yelling!	79
40	Trauma and Faith	81
41	Reading	83
42	Anger Management for Kids	85
43	Christian Fatherhood	87
44	Bedtime Habits	89
45	Divorce and Kids	91
46	Challenges That Come with Change	93
47	Sex and Gender Education	95
48	Teaching Kindness	98
49	A Checklist for Christian Parents	100

Foreword

Effective parenting in today's world is a monumental challenge. Good models are hard to find; there are almost as many parenting styles as there are parents. Many of the so-called experts who claim to promote parenting excellence do so from a purely humanistic perspective. And the messages that flow through the veins and arteries of our popular culture regarding the parental role are often shallow and misleading.

When *Lutheran Parent* began searching for the right person to write a column for the magazine, the bar was set high. Such an individual would be required to understand how precious children are, not only in the eyes of parents but in the eyes of a loving God as well. Furthermore, this writer would be expected to address some of the most difficult parenting issues with profoundly practical insight. And, as if the task of finding such an individual were not already difficult enough, each column needed to communicate a gospel-centered message with clarity, sensitivity, and in a generous, nonjudgmental tone.

The Lord's answer to *Lutheran Parent's* dilemma was typically over-the-top. In addition to fulfilling all of the aforementioned requirements in superb fashion, John Juern brought to the column an exceedingly high level of professional expertise and a reputation in the Lutheran community for having a deep understanding of children and their needs. This volume represents eight years of Dr. Juern's columns, proudly published on the pages of *Lutheran Parent* magazine between 1996 and 2004. It presents the difficult job of raising kids in today's world in a way that is thoroughly consistent with how Scripture portrays it . . . *in the shadow of Christ's cross.*

Kenneth J. Kremer
Editor

chapter 1
Obedience and the Heart

Why should children obey their parents? Ask different people and you get different answers: "They're supposed to . . ." or "I'm the parent!" or "If they don't, they'll be grounded." A Christian parent might reply, "The Bible tells children to obey their parents." And it does. But none of these responses gets at the real heart of God-pleasing obedience.

The answer to that question sets Christian children apart from others. Take away Christian faith, and a child's obedience is usually connected either to the fear of punishment or the promise of reward. For the Christian child, obedience to parents flows out of a love for Jesus. All of us as Christians—adults or children—do what we do because it's our way of showing our gratitude for all that the Lord has done for us, beginning with his gracious gift of salvation. The Bible says it this way: "We love because he first loved us" (1 John 4:19).

This is a fundamental principle: We obey God by living according to the Ten Commandments, and we live that Christian life out of love for him. So, the essence of all Christian discipline is serving the Lord with our lives.

Loving the Lord doesn't happen on its own. The Holy Spirit plants the seed for such an obedient life at the moment of Baptism. And God is with Christian parents every day as they teach children that misbehavior and disobedience are sins. It's really quite simple: Christian parents teach their children that wrong is wrong because it ignores God's Ten Commandments.

But along with teaching children right from wrong, parents need to tell their children about the wonderful gift of forgiveness that is theirs through faith in Christ Jesus. Their sins are forgiven. That forgiveness brings joy. And the joy is expressed in the children's obedience. It's that message of forgiveness that motivates them.

Yes, a child will sin again. And probably again and again. But each time, there is forgiveness and joy and a renewed commitment to do God's will.

Parents don't need to go through this explanation every time their child does something wrong. The key is to remain consistent with God's will in setting rules and expectations for children; let the Ten Commandments set the standard.

There is still an appropriate time and place for time-outs, grounding, other types of punishment. Sin has consequences. Star charts posted on the refrigerator door and surprise hugs can still reinforce good behavior. But these things in and of themselves do not bring about compliant behavior. Christian children obey their parents because they love their Savior.

chapter 2
Responsibility and Kids

Children are not born with a natural inclination to be responsible. It doesn't suddenly appear at age 12 or in the first year of high school or when a teen gets a driver's license. Children learn responsibility by being taught it, by practicing it, and by observing it in their parents. When we fail to teach responsibility, we are, in reality, teaching children to be irresponsible.

Already at two years of age, a child can be taught to put toys away, put dirty clothes in the basket, carry plates and cups to the sink after a meal. At this early age, children do not make a distinction between work and play. They are eager to do the same things that grown-ups do. But they don't have the necessary skills, so a parent will have to do the activity with the child instead of just telling him or her what to do.

As children grow older, they can be taught to answer the phone properly, wash and put away dishes, clean up after pets, fold and put away clean clothes, and a lot of other common, everyday tasks. Children need to have jobs that are a part of their daily routine to learn the importance of routine and consistency. They need to learn that everyone in the family does a share of the work. Paying a child for routine jobs emphasizes materialism and does not provide an opportunity to learn the concept of serving. In giving children opportunities to do tasks around the house, the goal is not perfection or speed; the goal is learning responsibility. When a parent is more concerned about getting the job done right or getting it done quicker than about teaching responsibility, it's unfortunate. As children learn to be responsible, they also develop self-confidence because they are experiencing success.

Children also learn about responsibility as they observe how their parents handle responsibility. They begin to understand a proper balance between work and free time. A workaholic parent, by example, teaches an inappropriate lesson about responsibility. A parent who frequently complains about his or her job will send a negative message to a child about work. Conversely, parents who share the joys of their work with their children communicate a positive work ethic.

A child who learns responsibility benefits from a positive self-image, but more important, the child and the parents share in developing their God-given gifts. After all, the ultimate reason for learning to become a responsible person is to give glory to God.

chapter 3

Trust and the Parent-Child Relationship

All relationships are based on trust. Children want and need to trust their parents. Parents want (and need) to trust their children. Trust makes honest communication possible; it builds relational bridges; it gives meaning to our respective roles; it provides security; it stimulates responsibility and caring. If a child never learns to trust, the results can be devastating.

In spiritual terms, we are born with a sinful nature that makes us unable to trust in God on our own. Only when the Holy Spirit has worked his miracle of faith in the heart of a sinner through Word and sacrament does the sinner have the capacity to trust in God's promises. Jesus' life, death, and resurrection are the central truths to which God's people cling for their well-being. Jesus himself said, "Do not let your hearts be troubled. Trust in God; trust also in me" (John 14:1). So our trust in God comes also as a gift from God. Without it we would be both hopeless and comfortless.

In human terms trusting isn't a natural reflex either; it must be learned. Even the world of psychology recognizes that children are born without the ability to trust. Developmentally, children learn to trust as they bond with their parents. A child who has never bonded tends to become an insecure, untrusting adult.

The bonding process begins already in the womb. As an unborn fetus identifies with the voice of its mother and as her body nurtures the child she is carrying, a bond is being established between mother and child.

After birth, as a mother cares for, holds, feeds, talks to, and in general interacts with her child, the child's overall sense of stability and predictability is established. If a mother is not emotionally available to a child on a consistent basis, that binding attachment which helps to establish trust is not there.

Soon a child is ready to begin to generalize that trust to others. A child's loving, trusting relationship with his father is important because a father-child relationship (albeit an imperfect relationship among two sinful people) is an earthly representation of the relationship between a child and his or her heavenly Father. A father who is absent, unloving, or overly critical becomes a stumbling block for his child, making it difficult for the child to comprehend a loving heavenly Father.

Many adults have had to overcome childhood experiences that undermined their trust. Parents who extend their love to a child with forgiveness, honesty, and compassion are helping their child learn to trust people.

chapter 4

Spanking

Today most child-rearing experts argue that children should not be spanked. It's probably a knee-jerk reaction to the growing concern about physical abuse in families. The feeling is that spankings only teach a child to become physically aggressive. Of course, few if any child-rearing experts refer to God's Word for guidance and direction in arriving at their opinion. If they would, they would learn that spankings are neither forbidden nor commanded in Scripture. But Scripture does leave the door open for parents to use spanking as an appropriate form of discipline under certain circumstances.

Texts like Proverbs 13:24, "He who spares the rod hates his son, but he who loves him is careful to discipline him," have been interpreted by some to suggest that spankings are encouraged in Scripture. Others point out that the rod spoken of in these texts is a shepherd's rod, which was used only to gently prod and encourage. Whether we are speaking of physical punishments or verbal reprimands, Scripture is clear in stating that all Christian discipline is to be carried out with love, never out of anger or for revenge (Colossians 3:12).

Depending on how it is administered, a spanking can still be an effective part of Christian training. Along with verbal reprimands, setting consequences, and speaking words of encouragement, spankings are part of the array of disciplinary tools available to help Christian parents shape the will of their child.

Here are a few things to consider as you decide how spankings might fit into your parenting style.

- ✝ Before administering a spanking, pray for wisdom and guidance.

- ✝ While a spanking should be close in time to the offense, a spanking should never be given if the parent's emotions are out of control.

- ✝ A spanking is a teaching opportunity. Make sure the child knows the reason for the spanking.

- ✝ Consider a child's age. He or she may be too young to make the connection between the behavior and the spanking. Or a child may be too old for the spanking if that action only creates resentment.

- ✝ Spankings should always be given on a child's bottom. Use your hand, nothing more. A slap on the face is not a spanking. If you find yourself using spanking as a threat, it is no longer a punishment reminder; it has degenerated into a symbol of power. Escalating frequency or the severity of spankings is another warning sign that spankings may no longer mean what you originally intended them to mean.

- ✝ Reserve spankings for defiant behavior. If a spanking is used for every form of misbehavior, it loses its effectiveness.

- ✝ Following the spanking, a child needs to be reassured of a parent's love and God's forgiveness.

chapter 5

Honesty

God made people to be truthful and honest in all things. But Satan, the father of lies and chief of dishonesty, seduced us into sin. Man's sinless and perfect nature was replaced with sin and all that is bad. By nature a child will lie, cheat, steal, and in general, be dishonest. David clearly stated, "Surely I was sinful at birth, sinful from the time my mother conceived me" (Psalm 51:5).

So, how does a child learn to be honest?

Parents must teach children what it means to be honest. Children are not born with that knowledge. The best way to teach honesty is to be honest. To a great extent, children become what their parents are. So parents must take care not to confuse children by giving a "do as I say, not as I do" example.

Help children understand the difference between playtime make-believe and lying about real issues. Creativity needs to be fostered, but not at the expense of truthfulness. While both are sinful, the deliberate, malicious, and defiant lie is more troubling than the impulsive, immature response of a child.

When a child chooses to be dishonest, try to determine why that choice was made. While dishonesty is always a sin, knowing the motivation behind the lie is helpful in teaching a child how to avoid that sin in the future. Is the child lying because he or she is fearful of the consequences of speaking the truth? Parents need to stress the understanding and forgiving nature of their Savior. We all make mistakes. We all deserve punishment. But when we admit our mistake and receive forgiveness, we can all experience the removal of that guilt. Praise and thank children for being honest and truthful. We all like to receive recognition for actions that are out of the ordinary. And while we would like honesty to become a natural response, we know that it is a learned response. It needs positive reinforcement.

Finally, understand and teach children that being honest is not done out of a fear of punishment. As in compliance with all commandments, children are to be truthful out of love for the Lord. They need to know, "I show love for Jesus by being honest."

chapter 6

Compulsive Lying

All children lie at one time or another. It's so easily done. Often it's not even noticed. Nevertheless, it is a sin. God demands honesty and truthfulness. Children lie because their sinful natures incline them to lie. While that is certainly true, it also raises the question of why some children are particularly prone to the sin of lying. Why does a child become a compulsive liar—one who is driven to lie repeatedly without any sign of remorse?

Very often children lie because they are copying parental behavior. Parents teach more by example than with words. The child who sees a parent lie learns that lying is appropriate behavior. Some parents actually encourage their children to lie. For example, a parent teaches lying by telling a child who is about to answer the phone, "If that's Mr. Smith, tell him I'm not home." Compulsive behavior in adults can become a template for compulsive behavior in children.

Sometimes a child will lie to fulfill unmet emotional needs. Exaggeration and fantasy stories fit into this category. They are ways of seeking recognition; they make the child feel important. Perhaps the child wants someone to listen and to pay attention. The object of this type of lying is to gain some kind of status.

Some children lie because they are more afraid of what might happen if they tell the truth. Perhaps they are so afraid of parental anger that they lie in an attempt to escape it. They may be afraid that their wrongdoing will be found out. They may also be afraid of an anticipated consequence—punishment, someone's wrath, or the loss of a parent's love or respect.

A parent cannot ignore the lies of a child. But while the lie itself must be dealt with, a parent must look deeper, below the surface, to try to understand why a child chooses to lie.

It is important to get at the root cause of the problem. Here are a few suggestions to help parents develop healthy attitudes regarding lying.

- Teach children that God expects them to be honest in all things. And being honest is a way of showing love for Jesus.

- Praise children for being honest, especially when lying would have been easy.

- If you know for certain that a child has lied, confront the lie.

- Look beyond just punishing lies, and try to determine why the child felt the need to lie.

- Children need to know of God's unconditional love and his forgiveness. Use such opportunities to remind your children that Jesus loves them and died to forgive the sin of dishonesty too.

chapter 7

The Twos

Bradley was finally in bed, sound asleep. He looked like a little angel. Quite a contrast to his waking hours when he is loud, curious, and volatile—a machine, constantly moving. Welcome to the world of the two-year-old—a time of significant learning, strong wills, and temper tantrums.

A toddler's developmental process gives special meaning to the phrase "fearfully and wonderfully made." This is a time of great physical development, language acquisition, intellectual curiosity, and emotional development. It can also be a time of frustration, anger, precious moments, and loving interaction for both parent and child.

For the first time in his life, a child now has the capability to explore his environment. He wants to run, jump, and kick. He wants to pick things up to see how they feel. He is curious about how drawers can be pulled out and books taken off shelves. This is all normal behavior. It allows a child the chance to further develop physical skills and cause-effect thinking. Parents need to encourage this process by actively playing with their two-year-old.

At this age, silence is definitely not golden. Parents need to talk with their child. During this time, a child learns to connect things with words, and he begins putting words together to express ideas.

By the end of the second year, a child has a vocabulary of about a thousand words. Words like *no* and phrases like *me do it* are a testimony to the two-year-old's spirit of self-will. But expressions such as *I love you* also find their way into his communication.

Two-year-olds express their emotions quite strongly. Their personality and character traits seem to really come out during this year. Self-gratification is usually the driving factor. At this age, children can use newly developed motor skills to express their anger by redecorating your walls. A two-year-old can also be downright stubborn, shouting "I don't want to" at the most embarrassing moments. Temper tantrums are a normal reaction to frustration. Parents can handle a tantrum best by letting it run its course, making sure the child is in safe surroundings and won't hurt himself or someone else. Don't give in; that will only reinforce such behavior. Stay calm. Be in control of yourself. Reacting with emotion to your child's emotion will only spawn more outbreaks.

A two-year-old's imagination also comes to life. Without hesitation, he imagines being a policeman, a tree, a dog. Imagination sows the seeds of creativity. It allows a child opportunities to "try on" different roles in life.

This is also a wonderful time to make up prayers and sing new songs to Jesus. Children quickly learn to retell Bible stories, often using pictures. They need to be encouraged to express their simple, child's faith in Jesus.

Two-year-olds always present some unique challenges for their parents. But the twos don't have to be a terrible time. This should be a time for unwrapping wonderful new experiences, feelings, and abilities that God has arranged for two-year-olds and parents to enjoy.

chapter 8

The Fantasy World of Children

How invigorating a child's imagination can be! In the world of fantasy, a child is able to become an astronaut, a nurse, a basketball star, or a missionary to Africa. Pretending allows children to travel, to have superhuman strength, or to have an imaginary friend named Fred.

Parents sometimes become concerned, however, about their child's ability to distinguish reality from fantasy, or they become afraid that their child pretends too much and will grow up unable to function effectively in the real world. For the most part, those fears are unfounded. Fantasy play gives children the opportunity to integrate elements of the real world into their world of make-believe. At such times, toys can help a child engage in the game of Let's Pretend. Parents can guide fantasy play by selecting suitable toys for their child. Such toys enable children to drive a car, prepare meals, build a house, fly an airplane, or put out a fire.

Fantasy play can also allow children opportunities to imitate various role models: a teacher when playing school, a pastor when playing church, a mother or father when playing house, a doctor when playing hospital. Such role-playing emphasizes the need for positive role models. It encourages children to see things from a different point of view. Fantasy play sharpens innovative instincts and prepares children for life in an adult world that places a high value on creativity.

There are also some negative aspects to fantasy play. Sometimes children fantasize getting even with those who have been hurtful to them. Such fantasy thinking is allowing sin to have control. The type of fantasy in which one is able to inflict harm on another needs to be addressed and discouraged. In today's world electronic games frequently foster a type of fantasizing that can involve violent behaviors; physical, emotional, or even sexual abuses; and other godless activity. Parents do well to being alert to these trends and monitoring their child's electronic game choices.

Although it is quite rare, occasionally the reality of life is so painful that a child retreats into a world of fantasy to escape. This may occur in children who suffer significant amounts of abuse. After time, the world of fantasy becomes their reality. Using fantasy to escape unpleasant realities also needs to be addressed.

God gives us an imagination to enrich our lives. He wants us to develop our creative instincts, using the Ten Commandments as a practical curb and guide. When we encourage our children to use their imaginations through fantasy play, we can help them glorify God's name.

chapter 9

Treating Attention Deficit/ Hyperactivity Disorder

When a child has been diagnosed as having an Attention Deficit/Hyperactivity Disorder (ADHD), medication is often prescribed. Unfortunately, many people view medication as the total treatment for ADHD. On the other hand, some view medication as unnecessary or even dangerous. Between these two extremes—medication alone or no medication at all—lies a safe path.

Medication does not cure ADHD; it treats the symptom of inattention. With medication the child will have greater attention and concentration ability. This will make it possible for a child to learn more easily and to better control behavior. It can be a very safe and effective tool for overcoming the effects of ADHD.

The three most commonly used medications for treating ADHD are Ritalin, Dexedrine, and Adderal. All three are actually stimulants. They are very powerful and must be used judiciously. Strattera, a nonstimulant, is also available.

Medication should never be looked upon as the total treatment for ADHD. Discipline techniques that make appropriate use of both law and gospel are fundamental to all Christian child-rearing. Structure, routine, consistency, and love must always be in place. Of these two approaches—medication or proper discipline—the latter is the more important because it trains the child. Medication only treats a symptom.

As with any medication, there are side effects. The most common side effects of those medications mentioned include loss of appetite, sleeplessness, headache, and upset stomach. These side effects usually disappear within two weeks after starting the medication.

There are also side effects of not using medication. A child who has significant ADHD and does not use medication will likely continue to have problems at home and in school.

Some believe that ADHD can be treated effectively by using a dietary approach. The Feingold diet, which is an allergy-elimination diet, is perhaps the most popular. However, the medical community tends to view this approach as ineffective, claiming that any positive effects of the diet are due to a placebo effect—it works because you believe it will work. Yet the diet approach has worked for many children.

Whether a medication or diet approach is used, Christ-centered discipline is the essential element. It alone creates the consistent, structured environment in which Christian children can grow in a God-pleasing manner.

chapter 10

Teaching Problem Solving

Just as adults face various problems every day, so do children. Children learn to solve their problems by watching parents react to their problems and solve them. But beyond the good example that every parent hopes to set, there are a few other things we can do to enhance the problem-solving power of our children.

† Don't shield your child from every problem that comes along. And certainly don't solve every problem for your child. Children need the experience of facing and dealing with difficulties on their own. It helps them grow in self-confidence, and it encourages them to go to God for the help and strength they need to attack their problems.

† Always take your children's problems seriously. Never laugh at them or make light of the problems they face. While you may not see the significance of finding a lost toy or not being invited to a party, your children view such problems as major crises. Children's problems are as real and as serious to them as are the problems parents face.

† Take advantage of a problem situation to teach valuable lessons. Assure your child that problems are not God's way of punishing us. In fact, just the opposite is true. Our problems are part of God's loving plan for us. They teach us to return to him

for help and strength. Don't miss these precious opportunities to teach that God is always in control, that nothing ever happens without his knowledge. Teach that "In all things God works for the good of those who love him" (Romans 8:28). (When you teach that wonderful truth to your child, your own faith will be strengthened as well.)

✝ Encourage your children to talk about the problems they face. Help them see all the options. Urge them to think out loud about where each option will lead. Teach them to talk to God, asking for guidance to make a wise decision—one that will give glory to his name. That, after all, is what every Christian ought to strive to accomplish.

✝ Teach your children to trust that God has led them to make right decisions. This is also an important part of decision making—learning to live with decisions we've made—to have the confidence that our choices will lead to God's own good purpose.

Dealing with problems is as much a part of everyday life as is sleeping and eating. The ability to effectively deal with life's problems does not come automatically; it must be taught. And when your children know that they are solving their problems in a God-pleasing way, it is also much easier to remember to thank God for his help and guidance.

When Parents Are Afraid to Parent

The two sons of the Old Testament priest Eli needed correction. They were sinning, and Eli knew it. He told them to stop; they didn't. At this point we are told that Eli "failed to restrain them" (1 Samuel 3:13). For whatever reason, Eli didn't follow through on his parenting responsibility. He quit. Maybe he thought they would stop on their own. Perhaps he believed they were going through a phase. Maybe he was afraid they would be angry with him if he disciplined them. Eli was older; perhaps he was too tired to discipline his sons. We don't know what went through Eli's mind. We only know he didn't do what God expected him to do.

As we look at parents today, some seem to fall into the trap of being afraid to parent. They know their child is doing something wrong, but they ignore it or blame it on someone or something else. Perhaps they refuse to deal with the problem out of fear that the child will rebel even more. Some parents may not want to deal with a problem because they feel they just don't have the time to deal with it. They may feel it's not a big deal; their child will grow out of it. Or perhaps the child's misbehavior creates a sense of guilt in the parent—"It's all my fault." For whatever reason, some parents seem to be afraid to discipline their children.

God's Word is clear about what he expects parents to

do for their children. "Train a child in the way he should go, and when he is old he will not turn from it" (Proverbs 22:6). This is both a command and a promise. The Bible also tells us that parents are to bring up their children "in the training and instruction of the Lord" (Ephesians 6:4). That is an expectation—God's expectation. But he also promises to help parents carry out that responsibility.

Our children are wonderful earthly blessings from God. May our response to God's love be one of thankfulness that seeks to raise God-loving children.

God has provided parents with tools and techniques to use in parenting. Here are a few that apply:

- Talk with your child, and be a good listener.
- Encourage your child.
- Recognize and compliment good behavior.
- Use the Ten Commandments to set clear and appropriate limits of behavior.
- Establish consequences for inappropriate behavior and stick to them.
- Always assure your child of God's and your unconditional love and forgiveness.
- Control your emotions. Don't allow a lack of self-discipline to become the problem.

chapter **12**

Time-Outs

Solomon could have been addressing every Christian parent when he wrote, "Pleasant words promote instruction" (Proverbs 16:21). His words are certainly worth contemplating. They encourage us to notice our children behaving properly and to let them know we are proud of them when they do. Solomon's words remind us to make sure our criticisms genuinely help our children and are not designed to put them down.

Children need to know what expectations we have set for them. They also need to know what consequences to expect if they do not behave according to those expectations. Time-outs, privilege limiting, and grounding are effective forms of discipline because they provide opportunities to talk about your expectations and the consequences for ignoring them.

Time-outs, such as the "thinking chair" or standing in a corner, work well with younger children. Time-outs should be relatively brief—about a minute or so for each year of age.

Limiting privileges works well with children of any age. Some privileges that can be limited include TV viewing, playing with a favorite toy, using the phone, or using the car.

Grounding is a useful technique with older children. Teens can be grounded to the house, grounded on weekends, or denied specific activities.

The key is to use the time to point out what your child is doing wrong and to explain what kind of behavior is expected. Also explain how the consequence will serve as a reminder for the next time a similar temptation arises. The choice is still up to the child. Then wait patiently for changes in behavior.

Look for positive changes. When you are able to see evidence of a change, tell your child you appreciate the change and are proud of his or her decision. If behavior doesn't change, the consequences may have to be administered again.

These little heart-to-heart talks also give you the advantage of planning how you will handle the situation. You will not have to come up with a consequence while you are upset. And you can think about how to reassure your child of your love and forgiveness.

All this occurs, of course, within the context of prayer. Everyone in the family can be included. Ask God to give you wisdom, patience, and understanding as you administer discipline. Ask God to bless your children by helping them learn from your patient and loving instruction.

chapter 13

Do Your Children Know You Love Them?

Christian parents show love for their children by providing for their spiritual needs. They teach their children about Jesus—his loving sacrifice on Calvary to win salvation for them. And they discipline their children, using God's Word to guide and direct behavior.

Giving time and attention to your children also shows your love for them. Parents need to be involved, spend time with their children, talk and listen to them, share their dreams and ideas. Some people promote the idea that the quality of the time spent together will make up for not spending much time together. Children need both, quality time and a large quantity of it.

While children do realize parental love from the things parents do for them, they also need to hear it. Hearing "I love you" makes adults feel special. These words do the same thing for children. Learn how to put your love into words. High drama isn't the objective. Nor are emotional displays. Simple communication is the whole point. Any time. Any place. Just say it: "I sure am happy that God gave you to me!"

Children also understand love through physical signs of affection. When mothers brought their children to Jesus for his blessing, Jesus not only spoke the words of blessing, he also gave a physical sign. We are told he "placed his hands on them" (Matthew 19:15). Children need to have hugs and kisses. They need to cuddle and wrestle. Obviously, as they get older, the forms of physical affection will change, but the need for it does not.

Some parents shy away from giving physical signs of love to their children. They say they are not a demonstrative family. Some fathers are particularly reluctant to show physical affection to their children, fearing that it will be misinterpreted. When this occurs, both parents and children are missing out on a wonderful experience. The appropriate physical affection of a father shows the soft side of his love.

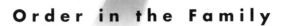

chapter 14

Order in the Family

"Everything should be done in a fitting and orderly way" (1 Corinthians 14:40). You agree, but you know this passage was not directed at families. It was directed to Christians to maintain orderliness in the worship service. Still, it can have an application to family life in the Christian home.

Our God is a God of order—be it in the way we worship, the orderliness of the laws of science, or the order in the home. God established order in the family when he created a structure for family life. Fathers are the heads of households. The father shares this role with his wife, and they are responsible for the running of the home. Parents are in charge. They carry out their responsibility out of love for their Lord and their children. Knowing this order in the family creates a feeling of stability and a sense of security for children.

Structure is a key part of family order. Families need structure because it establishes responsibility and accountability within the family. It determines who is to do what in the family setting. And the roles created within a family structure set behavioral expectations for children and parents alike.

Another part of order is routine. Families do well and children feel secure when there is a predictable daily pattern for getting things done. Routine suggests a regular time for getting up, going to bed, eating a meal, doing homework, or practicing the piano. Regular, daily routine gets things done because it brings about self-discipline.

In our society establishing a daily routine is a challenge. Contrary to what many parents believe, routine does not limit activities; rather, it organizes them. While there does need to be flexibility in scheduling and times for spontaneous activities, daily routine is basic for getting things accomplished.

Here are a few suggestions to help bring some order into a hectic schedule:

- Have a large calendar that lists all family events.

- At the beginning of the week, review with the family the events of the week.

- In the morning review the events of the day with your children. Let them know what is planned for after school and the evening hours.

- Teach children how to plan their activities for a day. (This can also have the added benefit of eliminating boredom.)

- Consistency is also a part of order. Consistency means that the rules, expectations, routines, and responsibilities remain the same from day to day. Consistency creates security because children know what is expected.

chapter 15

Attitudes about School

Some children seem to naturally love school and enjoy doing the work. Others see school as a chore and are easily frustrated with it. Most children probably fall somewhere between these two extremes.

Favorable attitudes need careful nurturing. The Bible tells us, "Pleasant words promote instruction" (Proverbs 16:21). Here are nine worthwhile ideas to help parents put that truth into practice.

- Let your children know you expect them to do well in school. They don't have to get straight A's. But let them know you expect them to use the gifts God has given them. This includes expecting them to pay attention, do the work on time, and be respectful to the teacher. Make it clear they are to obey the teacher as they obey you.

- Show interest in your children's work. Know what the social studies unit is about. Learn about the science experiments done in class. Review the Bible history lesson. Inquire with genuine interest, not as an interrogation. Look at papers. Show interest in your children's ideas. Dads need to be involved in homework too so that children won't view homework as just a "Mom thing."

- Be realistic about your children's abilities. Don't expect above-average work from a child with average abilities. Praise and encourage the child who finds learning difficult and frustrating.

- Be aware of concepts and facts that may need to be reviewed or re-taught. Quite often, a little more review or practice of a new skill will help improve it.

- Encourage your children to do neat work. If you notice that schoolwork is becoming sloppy, let your children know that if their work does not improve, they will need to do it over.

- Provide a regular time and place for doing homework. Be available during this time to offer help and encouragement, but do not do the work for your children. Avoid sitting down next to your child. If that is done on a regular basis, he or she may expect you to sit there for every homework session.

- Don't work past the point of frustration. If either you or your child becomes emotional, stop and take a break.

- Make sure homework comes to an end. The entire evening cannot be spent doing homework. There may be times when homework time needs to end before all the homework is done.

- Maintain regular contact with your child's teacher. Positive communication will go a long way toward a successful school experience.

chapter 16

Crime and Consequence

Every child must learn to take responsibility for his or her wrong behavior. Just as Adam wanted to blame Eve and God for his sin, so children like to blame others when they do wrong.

Consequences are needed as a follow-up to godless behavior. Consequences serve as a reminder that we are accountable. While God forgave Adam and Eve's disobedience for Jesus' sake, he still banished them from the Garden of Eden. The consequence for their sin was an expression of God's love for them, as well as an expression of his disgust with sin.

A five-year-old who refuses to pick up his toys when told may need to have his play with those toys restricted for a few days. A ten-year-old who always seems to dawdle instead of getting ready for school may need to miss her breakfast. A 13-year-old who is not applying himself faithfully and getting poor grades may need to lose phone or TV privileges until the grades improve. A 17-year-old who comes in after curfew may need to be grounded for a weekend or two.

Setting appropriate consequences for improper behavior is a very important parenting tool. Knowing what kind of consequences are appropriate for bad behavior is important for parents to learn. In deciding what consequences are appropriate, consider the following points:

✝ Does the child know that the behavior is wrong?

✝ Does the child know what kind of behavior is expected?

✝ Does the child know what consequence will be applied for not choosing God-pleasing behavior?

If the consequence is set ahead of time, a parent will not have to determine an appropriate consequence while under the emotional stress caused by the bad behavior. Here are a few examples of consequences that fit the crime.

Crime	Consequence
messy room	no "fun activities" until the room is clean
sassy talk	"time out" in the corner or some other boring place
sibling conflict	a specific period of separation for both parties
morning lateness	get up a half-hour earlier
crabbiness	earlier bedtime

After a child has experienced the consequence, review the action that brought on the consequence. Explain that repeating the irresponsible behavior will result in the same unpleasant consequence.

Finally, assure your child of your love and Jesus' love and forgiveness. This is an opportunity for teaching. Make the most of it. Explain that the purpose of obedience is not to avoid unpleasant consequences but rather to show love for Jesus.

chapter 17

Learning and the Senses

Our brains constantly receive and interpret messages that come through our senses. The brain recalls a sound as a siren or the word *hello*. It can recognize the face of a friend or appreciate beautiful scenery. It registers the feel of a blanket as soft and cuddly. The taste of chocolate is different from that of a lemon. The smell of perfume cannot be confused with the smell of a skunk. The brain recognizes and stores all these sensations for future use. This is how new information gets into the memory. That all this takes place with little effort on our part is a practical example of how we are "fearfully and wonderfully made" (Psalm 139:14).

Because of our unique, God-given talents, individuals learn in somewhat different ways. Some children are primarily auditory learners. They learn best by hearing and talking about things. A visual learner likes to see what is learned. For the visual learner, a picture is worth a thousand words. The auditory learner prefers the thousand words. What about those children who always want to touch and feel everything? Some children need to be physically involved in learning. They need to touch and feel to learn. Some individuals are better at hands-on learning than book learning.

Each learner probably favors one learning mode over another. But all children, even adults for that matter, learn best when they can involve more than one of their senses. Our senses often complement each other. Can you imagine a chef relying solely on sight and not using the sense of smell or taste? That's why oral reading instead of silent reading is better for some children. Oral reading uses two senses, sight and hearing, while silent reading uses only one. Some children need to physically experience the new learning. They may need to manipulate the letter *F*, move buttons around to understand borrowing, or feel the vibrations that make sounds.

To assist your child in learning and understanding new material, try to present that material through as many senses as possible. The more senses the brain uses to process information, the more places the brain can store and access that information.

To make learning more fun and increase memory and understanding, wake up the brain by using a variety of methods that involve all the different senses.

chapter 18

Neuroscience

So, parent of an infant or toddler, what are you doing to help your child make lots of neural connections these days? Maybe you need to learn more about what you can do to help your child develop those all-important neural connections that bring about learning.

Neuroscience studies the brain and how it functions. It explains that through the workings of billions of nerve cells with trillions of connections, the brain receives stimuli, processes it, remembers a lot of it, and produces learning. Neuroscience demonstrates the complexity of the human mind and the wonder of God's creation. It supports what the psalmist observed for us long ago: "I praise [God] because I am fearfully and wonderfully made" (Psalm 139:14).

Neuroscience explains how a vast amount of learning takes place long before a child ever attends school. It also explains that some kinds of learning, like learning how to see and talk, may only take place at specific times during a child's development. It's clear that a toddler is not just passing time until school starts but is actively learning with every sight, sound, smell, and movement that he or she experiences. And in the process, the child is making plenty more of those important neural connections.

You can help your child develop visual connections in the brain by pointing out colors, faces, moving objects, and things like the little holes in Cheerios. Show how things move up and down, how a coin looks larger through a magnifying glass, and how small an airplane looks because you're far away.

Develop speech and language parts of the brain by regularly talking and reading to your child. As you talk, your child learns the sounds and structures of the language. Teach words—their meaning, their sound, their value. Regularly set aside time for reading. It's okay to read that favorite book over and over. It brings comfort. All these activities build connections between nerve cells and make neural pathways for other learning to follow.

Enhance musical and rhythmic connections. Teach songs to your child. Sing together. Sway. Stomp. Skip. Plod along to the rhythms of the music. Help nerve cells make lots of new connections by rocking, swinging, and doing the elephant walk. Crawl on the floor. Stand on one foot. Shuffle under a limbo stick to help your child learn how to balance. Encourage fantasy and creative play to help develop the creative part of the brain. In this way, you will be changing the structure of your child's brain. It's neuroscience.

chapter 19

Drugs and Alcohol

They know it's wrong. They have learned it is harmful. Why, then, do children still choose to experiment with drugs and alcohol?

Think of a hungry lion, stalking its prey—the weak and vulnerable—those who wander from the group. The beast selects a target and waits. That is how Satan operates (1 Peter 5:8). Our children are unprotected when it comes to dealing with the temptation to experiment with drugs and alcohol.

Thank God, Scripture also describes the model for Christian parenthood to counter Satan's efforts. "Fathers, do not exasperate your children; instead, bring them up in the training and instruction of the Lord" (Ephesians 6:4). But what exactly does that mean?

- ✝ Parents, do not cause your child to become bitter. Do not physically, sexually, or verbally abuse your child. Do not withhold your love. Don't be overly critical. Don't set unrealistic expectations. Do not expect your child to be what you were not. Don't make your child overly dependent on you.

- ✝ Bring your child up in a nurturing environment. Show your love in words and actions. Spend time with your child. Listen. Make an effort to understand.

✝ Train your child to behave in a way that gives glory to God's name. That kind of behavior flows out of love for the Savior and a desire to serve him. Such training includes being an example for your child to follow. Be a model of how drugs and alcohol can be used in an appropriate way.

✝ Instruct your child in God's Word. Hold family devotions. Pray with your child. Attend church together. Extend and expand your child's religious instruction and faith life by making use of agencies that provide Christian education. And then reflect the same religious training that your child receives in a Christian school or Sunday school in what you say and do at home.

A child who experiences this kind of love at home is less likely to look for recognition and acceptance in places that could prove dangerous.

But some parents have done everything humanly possible to help their children avoid these temptations, and their children have still fallen victim to the hungry lion's assaults. The parable of the prodigal son reminds us that some children will need to learn things the hard way. Parents of such children can find comfort in the hope that what they taught in their children's early years will still be at work in their hearts in later years.

chapter 20

Childhood Depression

It's hard to imagine that a child in grade school could be depressed. These years should be filled with friends, sleepovers, sports, and other fun activities. Can a child actually be depressed? According to some estimates, about 5 percent of school-aged children experience clinical depression.

The estimate is probably a reasonable one. All children have times when they are unhappy and withdrawn, but that is not depression. That's just a normal part of everyday life. A clinically depressed child experiences many of the following signs over a longer period of time:

- Frequent crying and prolonged times of sadness
- Feelings of hopelessness
- Loss of interest in activities
- Lack of energy
- Increased time spent in isolation
- Change in eating or sleeping patterns
- Talk of hurting one's self or others

Some children are more likely to experience depression than others. Those who live in families where there is much stress because of family discord may be more inclined to become depressed. Children with learning difficulties, behavior problems, or who have experienced the loss of a relative or pet may become depressed. Depression also tends to run in families.

Telling children experiencing depression to "cheer up" or "get over it" will not help. Such children have not chosen to be depressed. They need help, usually in specific ways.

- With a loving ear, listen to your child's worries. Give constant reminders that reassure him or her of your love and God's love.

- Make sure that it is clear that both your love and God's love are completely unconditional.

- Use these comforting words of Scripture: "Cast all your anxiety on him because he cares for you" (1 Peter 5:7).

- Ask your pastor to talk with your child. He or she may be troubled by a particular sin or possibly confused about a biblical teaching.

- Talk to your child's teacher. Find out if a problem is occurring in the classroom.

- Talk to your doctor about your concern. Some medical conditions can cause clinical depression.

- Seek professional help. Obtaining an accurate diagnosis will help to determine an appropriate treatment.

- Continue to pray for and with your child. Ask for God's comfort, wisdom, and direction.

- Finally, trust in God. He will lead you and your child through this difficult time and will bring peace and good from it.

chapter 21

Suicide

The teen years are not always the enjoyable, carefree time of youth. For some this may be a time of great anxiety, emotional turmoil, significant mood changes, and feelings of isolation, hopelessness, and helplessness. Some deal with these uncomfortable feelings by using drugs or alcohol or by sexually acting out. They are trying to numb out the hurt. Others hurt so badly they see suicide as the only way to stop the hurting.

Everyone feels down, blue, or sad some days. That's a natural reaction to events that occur in life. Failing a test, not being asked on a date by the right person, or losing car privileges disappoint and cause unhappiness. These hurt feelings go away with time. This is not depression.

With depression, the sadness, isolation, alienation, hopelessness, and helplessness become so intense and overwhelming that the person cannot function in a normal way.

While only a licensed psychologist or physician can diagnose someone with depression, the symptoms usually fall into similar patterns. They include change in sleep patterns, change in appetite, loss of physical energy, loss of interest and desire for activities, a significant drop in grades, a negative attitude toward self and others, and social withdrawal and isolation.

While not everyone who experiences depression is suicidal, suicide is always a concern. Because of the particular struggles adolescents experience, coupled with a typical idealistic (black/white) thinking, they tend to be susceptible to suicidal thoughts. Unfortunately, suicide is one of the leading causes of death among teenagers.

Some adolescents seem to be at greater risk for thoughts of suicide than others. The following seem to be at special risk:

- Those who have lost a close friend or relative to suicide.
- Those who use and abuse alcohol and drugs.
- Those who like to talk about suicide.
- Those who see no hope for the future.

Can Christian young people experience any of these feelings? They can, and they do. Christians are still human. Sometimes their weakness overpowers their faith. But Christians have an unlimited source of power at their disposal—the grace and mercy of a loving heavenly Father. A Christian is never completely alone to deal with those difficult times.

If you suspect someone (either child or adult) is depressed or suicidal, encourage him or her to get help. Ask that person to talk with a pastor who will be able to point out God's wonderful promises of help. But also encourage such people to seek appropriate medical help to begin to deal with their depression.

Finally, pray for those people. Those who are experiencing depression frequently don't even have the will or the energy to pray on their own behalf. So they need others to pray for them. Ask the Lord to provide them with help, healing, and protection. "The LORD is close to the brokenhearted and saves those who are crushed in spirit" (Psalm 34:18).

chapter 22

At Times of Loss

A death in the family can provide parents with a wonderful opportunity. What better time to teach your children the story of God's love for all people? The gospel brings great comfort at such a time—comfort that every Christian sooner or later learns to appreciate at the death of a believer.

There are all sorts of clinical reasons why people die; there is only one real cause of death: sin. "The wages of sin is death . . ." But death is not an end. Because of God's great love for all people, Jesus came into the world to forgive sins and lead the way to eternal life in heaven. ". . . but the gift of God is eternal life in Christ Jesus our Lord" (Romans 6:23).

Our society does not accurately depict death. In children's cartoons no one ever dies. No matter how many times Wile E. Coyote is run over by a steamroller, blown up by gunpowder, or falls off a cliff, he always comes back for more. The lesson seems to be that death doesn't happen. Some computer games teach children they can "outsmart" death by taking certain actions.

Generally speaking, children younger than five do not see death as final. Around the age of 6 or 7, a child begins to grasp the fact that someone who has died is not going to return. What a comfort to know that when people die knowing Jesus as their Savior, they are happy in heaven.

For many children, their first experience with death

may be the death of a grandparent. For some the death of a pet may actually be more difficult than that of a relative because they played with the pet every day. The death of a pet may cause a greater sense of loss. You can comfort your children at a time like this by assuring them that God will help them get through the pain and sadness. If they ask whether their pet went to "doggy heaven," you can say that there may be pets in heaven. We don't know. The Bible doesn't tell us. We can only be sure that in heaven our joy will be complete. The Bible is very clear on that last point.

With the death of a close relative, it is also important to realize that children will deal with it in stages. At first there may be a denial of the death or even anger about it. This is usually followed by a period of grief. That grief may very well recur at some future event, such as confirmation, a first date, or graduation from high school.

As children experience death:

- Encourage them to express their emotions. This is a time to cry and mourn.

- Plan to attend the funeral service, because it provides comfort.

- Talk about death. Children may really wonder, "Can grandma see us now?"

- Talk about the one who died. Tears may flow once again, but it is good to talk about pleasant memories, even if we cry.

- Look for pictures and keepsakes to help keep the memory alive.

- Don't give wrong information about death, such as "God needed another angel, and that is why Grandpa died."

chapter 23

Beyond Stress

Everyone experiences stress. Adults may be stressed by changing jobs, planning a vacation, buying a car, or having the in-laws over for a meal. Stress is neither good nor bad. It is simply the body's reaction to an event.

Very young children show their stress by crying. They cry when they are hungry, need to be changed, or are bored. They may also show visible signs of stress as a response to a loud noise, the face of a stranger, or a fear of falling.

Children younger than age 5 are often fearful of storms, animals, the dark, and separation from parents.

A child in the elementary grades may be fearful about being hurt, being robbed, being sent to the principal's office, or failing a grade. All these fears are quite normal and can be dealt with by reminding your child of God's love and protection. It helps to be specific and direct. Use God's promises: "Cast all your anxiety on him because he cares for you" (1 Peter 5:7), or "In all things God works for the good of those who love him" (Romans 8:28).

When stress begins to interfere with normal routine, anxiety or worry sets in. The fear of having to talk with people can progress to the point at which a child will talk to no one. Fear of the dark can grow to such proportions that a child needs to sleep with parents. The stresses associated with school can become so great that a child is unable to attend school.

Occasionally a child's fears are connected with unusual behaviors. For example, a child who believes the saying "step on a crack and break your mother's back" may become terrified of stepping on the cracks in a sidewalk. Another child may have to have everything in the room in its exact place before going to bed at night. Or a child may wash his or her hands repeatedly beyond the point of cleanliness.

Merely explaining that a fear is baseless usually does not eliminate the fear. Here are a few things that you can do to help your child deal effectively with anxiety:

- Assure your child of God's continued protection.

- Pray with your child, asking for God's help in overcoming the fear.

- Allow your child to talk about those things that are frightening.

- Plan events ahead of time. Making things predictable tends to decrease anxiety.

- Communicate your plans with appropriate detail.

- Develop a plan of action for dealing with a particular fear.

- Seek professional help if the fear persists and interferes with routine.

chapter 24

Potty Training

The questions begin when a child is about a year old: At what age should I begin potty training? Does a difficult experience cause emotional damage? What if my child refuses to be trained? These are common concerns. First-time parents find them particularly worrisome.

God's Word does not talk specifically about potty training, of course. But that doesn't mean we can't apply some biblical principles in general terms. The Bible does remind us, "I am fearfully and wonderfully made" (Psalm 139:14). The body grows and develops according to a set pattern that God determines. With children, the bones grow, muscles develop, and thinking matures all according to his plan.

Successful potty training cannot begin until the body has developed some specific muscular control. Most children, especially boys, do not have the necessary muscle control until age 18 months or later. Training before then will only frustrate both parents and child.

An observant parent will see signs suggesting that the time for training can begin. It may be a special look on a child's face. Or the child might move to a quiet corner for privacy.

Potty training should be carried out in a positive manner. Punishing or yelling at a child for accidents will only create tension and make the process more difficult. Positive statements from parents for good attempts at elimination are very helpful.

It is usually helpful to use a small potty. A child is able to sit on a small toilet for longer periods of time. Having a child sit on a large toilet may be too tiring for the parent and perhaps even a little scary for the child.

After a child has successfully gone on the potty, there needs to be a lot of verbal praise. A small, tangible reward, such as a few pieces of candy, is good positive reinforcement.

The next step is to move from diapers to training pants. Continued use of diapers may delay the process because the diaper confuses the message that goes from the nerves to the muscles.

It is also quite helpful to get your child into a potty routine. An observant parent will likely notice a pattern.

Daytime control is usually accomplished before trying to achieve dry nights. After a time, you may expect your child to help clean up an "accident," not as a punishment but as a way of teaching personal responsibility.

Remember, this is a learning process. Learning takes time and includes making mistakes.

chapter 25

Bed-Wetting

At one time or another, most children will wet the bed at night. That's to be expected. It is all part of the normal progression of learning and muscle training to master bladder control.

Rarely is bed-wetting the sign of an emotional problem. However, it may be a symptom of an emotional problem when it is associated with major stress factors occurring in a child's life.

Regular bed-wetting—even in older children—is more likely the result of a lack of physical maturation rather than a psychological difficulty. Children who regularly wet their beds at night have very likely not developed the necessary muscle control to inhibit the release of urine during the night. Or it could be that a child is such a sound sleeper that the signal coming from the bladder to the brain is not strong enough to wake the child.

Since a child's rate of physical maturation does tend to have a hereditary factor, it is not unusual to find that bed-wetting runs in families. If one parent was a regular bed wetter, there is about a 40 percent likelihood that his or her children will have some difficulty. If both parents struggled with bed-wetting as children, there is a 70 percent likelihood that their children will be bed-wetters.

Here are some ways to deal with regular bed-wetting:

- Deal with the problem in a calm manner. Negative reactions by a parent will usually make the situation worse.

- Do not attempt to start potty training until your child is developmentally ready for it. Bed-wetting is more likely to occur if potty training was started too early.

- Encourage your child to want to stay dry at night. It may be wise at first to offer some reward for a dry night.

- Always have your child sit on the potty before going to bed, even if he or she says, "I don't have to go." Remember, you are trying to develop a habit.

- Set limits on the liquids—especially avoid soda with caffeine—that your child drinks before going to bed.

- Don't expect dry nights until there are consistently dry days.

If bed-wetting continues on a regular basis over an extended period of time, consult a physician. If there is no medical problem, consider using a pad-and-bell device. This device wakes a child as soon as he or she begins to wet.

chapter 26

Spiritual Strength

All parents want their children to be successful. But Christian parents desire more than earthly success. We want our children to know Jesus as their Savior. We want them to spend eternity with their Lord in heaven. No other goal could be loftier or more important.

Here are six biblical principles that work in a godly family:

✝ Build upon the foundation of your marriage. The marriage relationship is the foundation for all other family relationships. A husband and wife who center their marriage on Christ are on their way to a God-pleasing family life. If the marriage relationship is strong, parent-child relationships will also grow strong and positive. A God-pleasing marriage relationship requires effort. Do not neglect it. If your marriage has fallen on hard times, build your future together as a family upon honesty, forgiveness, and love.

✝ Love your children. Christian love is part of everything you do. Tell your children that you love them and thank God for them. Jesus is the model we follow as we show our love for one another. As Jesus put his hands on the children and blessed them, parents need to give hugs and kisses to their children. Spoken and expressed love brings about a feeling of security.

- ✝ Teach your children about Jesus. While the Sunday school, vacation Bible school, and other agencies of Christian education are available to help parents, it is still the responsibility of parents to impress spiritual truths upon their children (Deuteronomy 6:6,7). Parents who teach their children about Jesus are pointing the way to heaven. Children can feel secure about their future when they know Jesus as their Savior.

- ✝ Talk with your children. Strive to "be quick to listen, slow to speak and slow to become angry" (James 1:19). Encourage the other members of your family, and remember that "pleasant words promote instruction" (Proverbs 16:21).

- ✝ Discipline your children in Christian love. Children need to have limits and know the expectations for their behavior. Set boundaries that are clear and fair. When the boundary is crossed, consequences need to follow. Christian discipline needs to be administered in patient love so as not to "exasperate" a child (Ephesians 6:4). The parent who "loses his cool" is not correcting the child but has added to the problem.

- ✝ Pray for your children. Pray for their worldly welfare, but especially pray for their spiritual growth and well-being.

chapter 27

Stuttering

It is not at all unusual for children to stutter as they begin to develop their language skills. Stuttering is so common during the preschool years that speech therapy is seldom recommended. Most young children who stutter outgrow it by age 7.

What is somewhat surprising is that even though stuttering is quite common, the cause of it is not totally understood. It is known that stuttering is more likely to occur in boys than in girls. It is also known that stuttering and other speech-related problems are somewhat hereditary. While stuttering is not caused by limited intellectual ability, it is common for children who stutter to have difficulties with reading and writing.

Stuttering is often made worse by parents and teachers who put pressure on the child, urging him or her not to stutter. Incidents of stuttering also increase when children feel stressed. It is even quite possible for children with very normal speech patterns to begin stuttering if there is an increase in the stress in their lives.

If stuttering continues past the age of 7 or if the stuttering is so severe that it interferes with a child's ability to communicate with others, an evaluation is in order. Most public school districts have a speech and language therapist on staff who is able to do such an evaluation. The family doctor may also be able to suggest the name of a speech pathologist.

For those children who do have a more severe form

of stuttering, there are specific forms of treatment available that will allow them to have a greater fluency in their speech.

Whatever the cause of the stuttering, some practical approaches are suggested:

- Be patient with the stutterer.
- Do not speak for the child.
- Do not laugh at or imitate the stuttering.
- Decrease family stress.
- Encourage the child to sing and do choral reading. Stuttering tends not to be a factor in these situations.

Finally, assure your child that he or she is loved by God and valued for who he or she *is*.

chapter 28

Negative Attitude

What parent has not been on the receiving end of a child's negative attitude? An attitude problem often shows itself in grumpiness, looks of disgust, and a general air of unhappiness. The apostle Paul knew about attitude problems when he instructed his friends in Philippi, "Do everything without complaining or arguing" (Philippians 2:14). What parents wouldn't be overjoyed if their children acted that way when told to do chores? Paul added that this kind of positive attitude comes out of love for the Lord.

Attitudes can be thankful or ungrateful, forgiving or unforgiving, loving or uncaring. A positive attitude does not happen on its own. Children learn about attitudes from their parents. When parents talk positively to each other, they model a positive attitude for their children. If children hear only complaining and negative thinking, they may grow up to be complainers.

Children also learn a positive attitude when they are able to see parents doing positive things, such as showing respect for others, demonstrating kindness, being generous, and exhibiting patience.

Love and encouragement from parents also build a child's positive attitude. When parents praise the appropriate behaviors of a child, rather than just criticize the negative behaviors, they are also cultivating a positive attitude in that child.

Besides being able to hear, see, and experience a positive attitude, a child must learn how to show a positive attitude. Paul told his Philippian friends to do things without complaining as a way of showing their love for their Savior. And he wrote to Christians in Corinth that whatever they did should be done "for the glory of God" (1 Corinthians 10:31). So parents need to tell their children that carrying out the garbage, drying the dishes, and making their beds are ways to show love for Jesus. That too is part of a positive outlook on life.

If your child frequently has an attitude problem, begin by looking at the attitudes you are modeling. Ask your child to tell you why he or she is unhappy, and describe the signs of a negative attitude that you are observing. Be prepared to listen. If the negative attitude continues to occur regularly, you may need to set some consequences for continuing to carry on with that attitude. And be sure to look for those times when your child shows a positive attitude, and praise and compliment him or her for it.

chapter 29

Narcissism

In Greek mythology, Narcissus was a handsome young man pursued by many young women. Because he rejected all their advances, he angered the gods. They decided he needed to be punished. His punishment was to fall in love with his image in a reflecting pool and thus never attain his heart's desire. The story is a myth, but narcissism—loving oneself above all else—lives on.

Narcissism comes naturally; it's part of our sinful, human nature. We are told in Genesis 8:21 that "every inclination of his [man's] heart is evil from childhood." Narcissism occurs in young children when they can only think of their own needs. With Christian training, a child learns to see Jesus as the most important person in life. A child also learns how caring about others and being sensitive to their needs can show love for Jesus.

Some children continue to be very narcissistic and may even continue that lifestyle into adulthood. They brag about their abilities and believe their accomplishments are greater than those of others. They lack compassion and find it difficult to put the welfare of others above their own. Their thinking can be summarized in the words "I am better than you are—I am #1."

Paul addressed narcissism when he wrote, "Do not think of yourself more highly than you ought" (Romans 12:3).

57

Narcissism is defeated when parents teach their children about Jesus' love for them. In the self-sacrificing love of their Savior, children have the perfect model to follow. As children learn of Jesus' love, they need to be taught how they can return that love. Parents teach love as it is based in real actions. As Paul outlined, "Whatever you do, whether in word or deed, do it all in the name of the Lord Jesus" (Colossians 3:17).

Parents need to train their children not to be self-centered—to help others and show concern for all. As parents model selfless love and demonstrate their concern for others, children learn a valuable lesson.

On the other hand, some parents foster their children's self-centeredness by overindulging them or continually protecting them from experiencing the consequences of their bad choices.

How tragic it is to spend a lifetime thinking only of one's self! How wonderful it is to live life for Christ by caring about others!

chapter 30

Birth Order

Is there a reason why over half of the US presidents, the majority of astronauts, and a large percentage of Rhodes scholars are firstborn children? Why is it that there is a high percentage of firstborns in the fields of medicine, law, and ministry? Why is it that firstborns tend to have high motivation and a strong need to achieve?

Firstborn children seem to have a head start on life when compared to subsequent children. This head start seems to follow them through life. Research shows that firstborns tend to walk and talk at an earlier age. For a time, the firstborn gets all the parents' attention, interest, and expectations. In response to all this individual attention, firstborns tend to be more responsible, better communicators, and more goal oriented. Also, parents often seem to have a more intense relationship with the firstborn than with other children.

Being firstborn, however, is not without its drawbacks. Because of their higher need to achieve, firstborns tend to experience more anxiety and frustration. Even as adults, they tend to be perfectionists or hyper-responsible in their daily activities. They are often more guilt prone than children born later in the birth order.

In contrast, by the time the youngest child comes along, parents are usually more relaxed and comfortable with their parenting ability. There are other children and other things to be concerned about. The rules may often be more relaxed, and day-to-day expectations may be lower. Since older children are available to take on responsibilities, the youngest child may become less responsible and more dependent. On the other hand, the youngest child may become more sociable and freer of stress because he or she is less likely to be competitive and achievement oriented.

In between these two extremes is the middle child (or children). This child often finds that, in any activity, the oldest can do it the best and the youngest can do it the cutest. There may be some jealousy at work. The oldest child is out there doing well, and the youngest is entertaining everyone. As a result, a middle child may feel left out. It often seems that middle children are searching for their particular "claim to fame" in the family. They establish their identity by filling a niche into which no other member of the family has become involved.

While birth order is fun to examine and interesting to speculate about, it is not all that important. What is important is that all children know they are loved by their parents . . . and their Savior.

chapter 31

Christian Discipline Is . . .

Thanking God for your child.

Teaching your child to pray.

Teaching Jesus songs.

Telling your child about Jesus' love.

Teaching your child how to be thankful for Jesus' love.

Telling your child you love him or her.

Expecting your child to show God-pleasing behavior.

Teaching your child to obey and honor those in authority.

Setting and enforcing limits.

Being a good role model for your child.

"Catching your child being good" and letting your child know you are pleased.

Teaching your child to be kind to others.

Giving your time to your child.

Expecting your child to do chores.

Talking with your child in a loving way.

Setting and following through on consequences for wrong behavior.

Being consistent and firm,
but not inflexible, with rules.

Helping your child memorize
important Scripture passages.

Asking God to protect
and bless your child.

Talking about Jesus
in daily conversation.

Telling your child what
you expect of him or her.

Continuing to pray for your child, even when he or she no longer lives at home.

The key to Christian discipline is found in the words of Proverbs 22:6, which says, "Train a child in the way he should go, and when he is old he will not turn from it."

chapter 32

Separation Anxiety

Little Sarah clings to her mother's leg on the first day of preschool. She sobs as her mother peels her off and seats her at the table.

Eight-year-old Bradley still will not go to sleep in his room at night. Every night he falls asleep on the couch and then is carried to his room and put into his bed. If he wakes up during the night, he crawls into bed with his parents. He panics whenever he is told to go to bed by himself.

Becky looked forward to her first sleepover. About 10 o'clock she calls and begs to come home because she feels sick.

Susan is forever following her mom around the house. At school she worries that her mother will get hurt or become sick and no one will be there to help her.

All these children have a disproportional fear of being separated from a parent. They may be experiencing what is termed "separation anxiety disorder."

The fear of being separated from a parent is natural. Infants cry when strangers pick them up. Toddlers show apprehension when their parents are not in sight. As children grow and mature, however, they learn that it's okay to be apart from their parents for a time—their parents will return and everything will be all right.

Some children, even as they grow older, have a very difficult time feeling comfortable when their parents are not in the immediate vicinity. Such children may feel panicky and scared. They may keep the uncomfortable feelings inside and develop physical problems such as headaches or stomachaches.

These problems can be difficult for family members to endure. The child may be very sensitive and well-behaved, and these emotional reactions seem out of character. Sometimes these problems occur within a family that is already struggling with some other form of anxiety.

If your child exhibits such fears, here are some things to consider doing:

- Listen to your child to try to understand his fears. Never ridicule him for being afraid.

- Make it clear to your child that you realize her fear is genuine.

- Assure your child of Jesus' ongoing love and protection. Review Bible stories and Bible passages that show God's protecting hand over all things.

- As much as possible, provide plenty of structure and routine for your child.

- In the morning, plan out the day's events with your child. This brings an element of predictability into her daily life.

- With prayer and loving encouragement, help your child face a particular fear with courage.

- If a particular fear continues to trouble your child over a period of time and disrupts normal family life, consider seeking professional help.

- Remember the power of prayer, and commit this situation to God's loving care.

chapter 33

Memorizing Scripture

Memorizing Bible verses, hymns, and catechism truths has always been a key part of Christian training. After giving the Ten Commandments, God instructed his people to take these truths and "impress them on [their] children" (Deuteronomy 6:7). What better way to impress these truths than to have them committed to memory!

Some children seem to be able to memorize very easily, while others seem to struggle. The following ideas may be helpful for parents whose children have a more difficult time:

- Explain the meaning of what is being memorized. If your child does not understand the meaning, memorizing will be more difficult. Knowing the meaning also helps a child apply the truth to life.

- The first part of actual memorization is to read or say the entire passage several times.

- Next, divide the passage into logical thought units. Explain each unit, and say the words of that unit several times. Keep working on that unit until it is known word for word. Have your child close his or her eyes and say it.

- Add the next thought unit to be learned. Explain it and repeat it several times. Then put both units together, and say it until it is memorized. Continue in this way by adding the rest of the thought units. Always go back to the beginning of the passage and repeat the words. Strive for exact, word-for-word memorization. After the passage is memorized, have your child explain what it means.

- Spread out the recitation work. Three 5-minute segments of practice will be more beneficial than one 15-minute session.

- If you or your child becomes frustrated with the memorization, stop and take a break. Anxiety blocks memory.

- When memorizing hymn stanzas, teach the rhythm of the poetry or memorize by singing the stanza.

- Some children may actually find it helpful to walk around the room as they memorize.

- Review memory work right before your child goes to bed. There will be better retention in the morning.

Memorizing God's Word is important not only because it provides instruction but because it also builds a treasury of support and comfort texts for use in times of need.

chapter 34

Compliant and Defiant Siblings

While all children are born sinful, some demonstrate their sinful nature more overtly than others. Some seem angry from birth. As they grow older, they challenge every rule placed before them. These children are often described as high-maintenance, defiant, strong-willed children.

Other children are less fussy as infants. They laugh and enjoy social interaction. Such children might be described as compliant, easy-to-parent, low-maintenance children.

The question is, What happens when you have one of each of these kinds of children?

You will probably find yourself treating each child differently. You may have different expectations for each child. The compliant child does routine chores without any hassle. The strong-willed child, on the other hand, balks at assigned tasks. The compliant child seems to require little attention, while the defiant child demands far more of your attention.

You may have to admit to having different expectations of each child. It may even happen that behaviors punished in the compliant child are seemingly ignored in the strong-willed child. With strong-willed children, it is often necessary to pick your battles since you cannot deal with every troubling behavior at once. At the same time, the compliant child will need to be taught to be forgiving of a sibling who is acting out.

This seems to have been the situation the father faced in the parable Jesus taught about a lost son (Luke 15:11-32). One son seemed very responsible and played by the rules. The other son was rebellious and strong-willed.

After squandering his inheritance, the rebellious son decided to return home to seek his father's forgiveness. The father welcomed him home with open arms; the past was forgiven and forgotten.

Part of Jesus' lesson is aimed at teaching us how our heavenly Father deals with our rebelliousness with forgiveness and mercy. But Jesus' parable goes on to show that the compliant brother was not forgiving. His problem was that he had built up anger and resentment toward his erring brother. He felt his father was being unfair to him by forgiving his brother. There is an added lesson here on how we should treat one another with forgiveness and love, instead of with jealous and judgmental hearts.

The story also points out that both strong-willed and compliant children need guidance and attention. Compliant children need to hear that good behavior is a way of showing love for the Lord, not simply a way of pleasing parents. They may also need to hear your explanation for why you seem to be giving more attention to their strong-willed siblings. Both types of children need to be reminded of God's law at times and of God's love and forgiveness at other times.

chapter 35

When Learning Becomes a Struggle

As a parent, you hurt for your child when learning becomes difficult. Perhaps word recognition skills have not developed, or reading comprehension seems to be very limited. Maybe those math facts just cannot be memorized, or the ability to write a readable sentence does not exist. You want your child to do well and wonder what you can do to make learning easier. If your child does experience learning difficulties, consider the following ideas:

- Begin your search for answers with prayer, asking for God's guidance and wisdom. Then talk to your child's teacher. Find out what difficulties the teacher sees. Consider the suggestions your child's teacher has to offer.

- Be certain there is no undiscovered physical problem. When was your child's last physical exam?

- Could he or she be experiencing a vision problem? If it's not a problem with visual acuity, could there be a problem with eye coordination? This is something to consider if you notice that your child's reading is choppy or if there is a tendency to skip over words or to lose one's place while reading.

- Could there be a hearing problem? This needs to be considered if your child has a history of ear infections. Hearing may not have gone through the normal developmental process, and as a result there may be difficulty hearing the differences in some letter sounds. If this is the case, your child will likely have difficulty learning to be a phonetic reader.

- Could there be other developmental concerns? Were there problems during pregnancy or early development? When were the various developmental milestones achieved? Could your child be a slower learner? If this is the case, you will find that he or she seems to fall a little further behind every school year.

- Could your child be experiencing a specific learning disability? This is something to consider if there is advancement in some academic areas and difficulties in others.

In order to find answers to these questions, it is often necessary to have your child evaluated. This type of evaluation is available through your local public school. Even though your son or daughter may not attend the public school, you may still make use of the school's diagnostic services. An evaluation will point out strengths and weaknesses in learning and give suggestions for solving problems.

Private tutoring is often one way to help your child improve in some basic skills. While the classroom teacher or school may be able to provide some tutoring, they may not be able to provide all the assistance that is necessary.

Don't assume learning will get better with time. Find out what's causing the struggle so that you can begin to understand how to help.

chapter 36

Homework Headaches

Many parents are confused over homework. Some wonder why their child seldom has any. Others have the entire evening centered on homework. All parents are concerned about how involved they should be in their children's homework.

Children benefit from having some homework on a regular basis. It gets them into the habit of setting aside time for study. There are some ways parents can navigate the maze of homework issues.

Do not get into the routine of spending two to three hours on homework every evening. On occasion parents may have to call it quits before all the homework is done. Neither children nor parents can work past the point of frustration. Homework time does need to come to an end.

Here are a few useful things to keep in mind:

- **Time:** Try to have your child do homework at the same time each school day. There is no best time to do homework, but the worst time to do it is right before bed.

- **Location:** It is also important to have a consistent study location. Some children do their homework sitting at a desk in their rooms. Others do better work at the kitchen or dining room table.

✝ **Television:** In spite of what they say, children cannot concentrate on homework while watching TV. Listening to music while doing homework may be less distracting, but it is still not a good idea.

✝ **Supervision:** Show an interest in your children's homework, but do not get into the habit of sitting down with them when they do their homework. If you do that on a regular basis, your children will make a connection between doing homework and having a parent as a crutch.

✝ **Plan:** For children who regularly have a lot of homework, plan out the order in which it is to be done. Have your child do the easier assignments first and save the harder things for last.

✝ **Reading:** If your child struggles with reading comprehension, have her or him read out loud. Oral reading increases comprehension because the material is processed through two senses. If your child has poor word recognition skills, read some of the material to her or him. Being able to listen to the assigned social studies text may help your child get through the material.

✝ **Review:** Help your child study for tests by orally reviewing the material together. Talk through the pictures and diagrams. Ask a lot of "why" questions. Regularly review spelling words, math facts, and memory work. Reciting memory work one more time before going to bed is helpful.

✝ **Encouragement:** Provide verbal encouragement. Children need to know that you appreciate their efforts.

★ **Contact:** Maintain regular contact with your child's teacher so you know how school is working out. Don't wait for the teacher to come to you if you see your child has a problem. If your child seems to have a lot of homework, talk to the teacher to see if he or she is using school time wisely.

chapter 37

Repeating a Grade

Is it ever wise to have a child repeat a grade? Or does retention create such emotional problems for a child that they outweigh any academic gains? This is a very difficult question. You need to consider several factors.

A major concern should be gaining an understanding of why your child is experiencing difficulty in the first place. The assumption that your child will automatically do better going through the same material a second time is a pretty big one. What if there is no improvement? Here's a better question: If our child repeats this grade, what will be done differently the second time around to ensure success?

The decision to retain a child is an action that needs to be well planned. And the planning should be done well in advance. Parents and teachers should already be discussing the possibility of retention by the middle of the school year. This is not the kind of decision that can be put off until the last few weeks. Furthermore, both parents and teacher need to be in complete agreement that retention is in the child's best interest. They must both have a clear idea of what each will do to make the next school year a successful one.

Generally speaking, it is best to retain a child in the earlier grades (kindergarten, first, or second grade). Holding a child back beyond that point may cause more emotional problems. For some children who struggle in kindergarten, it may be better to place the child into first grade with the common understanding from the start that the child will spend two years in first grade.

Oftentimes children are held back in school because they are immature. That term, however, can be very misleading. On what basis do you make such a judgment? The immature child is somewhat likely to be one of the younger children in the class and is likely to display more childish social behavior. He or she may not fit in as well with peers, preferring to interact with younger children. Often the so-called immature child is also more physically immature.

Several other things may also need to be considered. If your child has a specific learning disability, retention will not solve the learning problem. A child with more limited intellectual ability will also not necessarily gain from retention. The bright, unmotivated child will not gain from retention. Also, if a child is more than a year behind in the development of academic skills, retention will likely not help. Finally, if your child is experiencing emotional problems, retention should not be considered.

Family concerns also need to be considered. Will your child be in the same grade with a sibling? Are both you and your spouse in full agreement about retention?

For children who have average intellectual ability but for some reason have fallen behind, retention may be a wise choice. Perhaps they missed a lot of days in school because of sickness. Perhaps their transfer into a more challenging school requires them to take a little more time to catch up.

Retention should always be seen as a positive action to help a child learn. It should never be used as a punishment for doing poor work.

The most important step in the retention process is telling the child. Because this is a decision that the parents and the teacher make for the child, he or she will need reassurance of their love and concern. Parents need to tell their child that retention will help him or her have an easier time in school and that this decision is not intended as a punishment.

chapter 38

When Parents Argue

Some people believe that parents should never argue in front of their children. Others think it is good for children to see their parents arguing. They contend that children need to learn that people do argue. They may even reason that in this way children can learn to resolve conflicts.

The reality is that most children, at some point, will see their parents argue. Whether they learn a valuable lesson or experience worry will depend on what they see and hear.

Arguments can upset both adults and children. Children are especially vulnerable to emotional hurt from seeing their parents argue. They can develop feelings of anger, fear, and guilt. Anger—because arguments can disrupt family life. Fear—that a parent will walk out or that there will be a divorce and the family will dissolve. And guilt—because children may think they are the cause of arguments.

It is especially upsetting for children to see one parent physically or verbally attack the other parent. It is likewise hurtful for a child to be drawn into an argument or to be forced to take a side in the conflict.

Parents need to settle disagreements without yelling. They should send their children to another part of the house so they will not have to witness all that is said. Remember, parents always serve as role models to their children. Children learn both good and bad lessons by observing their parents.

Parents need to try to settle arguments as quickly and quietly as possible. And, as in all things, "Let your gentleness be evident to all" (Philippians 4:5). When the argument is over, children will look for some assurance that mom and dad have worked out their problem. This is also an excellent time for parents to pray with their children, asking God to bless the family by restoring its relationships to peace and harmony. Any parent who has violated one of God's commandments should apologize for words or actions that were not God pleasing.

Parents need to realize that their arguing is very likely a sign that their marital relationship is under stress. All parents need to work on their marriages. Strong marital relationships will produce solid foundations for positive family relationships.

chapter 39

Stop Yelling!

A frustrated parent says: "I hate yelling at my kids, but that is the only way I can get their attention. They're not bad kids. They just don't listen, and then I end up yelling."

It's true that the more you holler, the more you have to holler. Kids "read" your yelling. They may think, "I'm still safe, she hasn't used my middle name yet." Getting children to obey through yelling is not effective and not God pleasing. If continued, it builds resentment.

Children are not born with a desire to be obedient— just the opposite. They are born with sin. The earlier obedience and respect are taught, the more effective they will be. God says we are to "train a child in the way he should go" (Proverbs 22:6).

Teaching children to obey starts with learning the meaning of no and redirecting children toward good (read that God-pleasing) behavior. Obedience also develops as children are taught to help out. They can put dirty clothes in a basket and bring their cereal bowls to the sink. Teaching responsibility early is an important part of training.

Christian obedience does not come from fear of punishment; it flows from love for God. "This is love for God: to obey his commands" (1 John 5:3).

Part of training also deals with wrong behaviors. Setting specific consequences for bad behavior can be very effective, such as telling a sassy child: "You are not going to talk to me in that tone of voice. Talk nicely. If you choose to continue to use that tone of voice, you will sit for ten minutes." If you use this approach, your child knows what behavior is wrong and what behavior you expect. It also explains what consequence will follow should the wrong behavior continue. Using this approach lets you plan out your actions rather than coming up with a consequence when you are angry. Emphasize that your child "chose" to do what you forbid. The message is "You brought this consequence upon yourself."

When children are fighting, it usually does not work to yell at them to stop. It's also not effective trying to figure out who started it. Both parties see the event with a bias. What does work is to tell them to stop fighting and play nicely and that if they choose to continue fighting, they will be forced to take a time-out: standing in a corner, sitting on a "thinking" chair, or going to their rooms. When the time-out is over, review the situation, tell your children they're forgiven, and let life return to normal.

It's also important to make a point of "catching your children being good." This gives you a chance to let them know when you are happy with their behavior.

Yelling doesn't work. God's Word tells us, "Pleasant words promote instruction" (Proverbs 16:21).

chapter 40

Trauma and Faith

One of the most important of all parental responsibilities is to protect children from harm and shield them from disaster. But hardships and catastrophic events still happen. And Christians are not immune from such tragedies. It is only with faith in a loving, almighty God that one can effectively deal with trauma.

Crisis takes many forms. It can be of international proportion, like the devastation of September 11, 2001, or a family event, such as an accident, a bankruptcy, a family member's arrest, or a terminal illness. For a child, a crisis may be the death of a pet, a friend moving away, or not making the team. When crises come:

- Encourage children to freely express feelings and ask questions.

- Give honest answers, but admit that it is sometimes difficult to understand God's ways.

- Pray together. Prayer acknowledges God's control and allows children an opportunity to do something to help.

- If a national tragedy is televised, do not allow children to watch it over and over.

- Provide opportunity for rest and relaxation. Do other activities to get your minds off the tragic event.

- Look for opportunities to involve children in some positive action. Does money need to be collected? Can a card be sent or a picture drawn? Can a tree be planted as a memorial?

- Assure your children that because God loves them, he will bring good from the event (Romans 8:28).

Children are usually quite resilient. But these signs may be cause for concern:

- Difficulty sleeping
- Recurring emotional expressions regarding the event
- Regression to previous behaviors
- Inappropriate fear or excessive crying
- Excessive attachment and dependency

Consult a professional child counselor if you see evidence of several of these signs. Saint Paul wrote, "God is faithful; he will not let you be tempted beyond what you can bear" (1 Corinthians 10:13). In times when families of the unbelieving world despair, Christians find strength and hope in these reassuring words from Scripture. And they pass that hope on to their children.

chapter 41

Reading

The national organization Reading Is Fundamental has it right: reading certainly is fundamental to helping ensure a child's success in school. Poor reading ability affects every subject during the school day. Children with weaker reading skills often see themselves in a negative way. In school, no one looks forward to hearing a poor reader read.

Unlike talking, reading is not a naturally occurring process. Reading has to be taught. Generally speaking, the ability to read is taught in a systematic process over an 8- to 12-year period. The reality, however, is that many basics of reading are learned long before a child is formally taught the process of reading.

So, parents, what can you do to help your child become a skilled reader?

The most important thing you can do is to introduce your child to words and language right away. A child is never too young to be talked to, read to, or sung to. These activities are critical for future reading because they introduce a child to the sounds of the language. It is also important to use a variety of approaches to introduce sounds. Singing to a child introduces more sounds and exposes one to the rhythmic quality words may have. Using rhyming words and words that describe sounds further broadens a child's exposure to sounds. Your voice tones will help expand an interest in and attention to words.

As you read to your child, use a variety of books. There are thousands of children's books on the market, but don't forget to read stories from the Bible also. Using a children's Bible provides not only good reading but also an opportunity for the Holy Spirit to work through the Word.

Encourage your child to explore a wide range of vocal sounds. Tape record his or her talk and play it back. Teach your child simple songs and prayers using the name Jesus.

Sometime around the age of 3 or 4, a child will start to show an interest in letters. While it is good for your child to be able to identify the name of a letter, the sound of that letter is really more important. As a child becomes more familiar with this symbol-sound relationship, use two- and three-letter words to show how the individual sounds are put together to make a word. Another fun activity at this age is for you to say the individual sounds of the letters in a word and have your child say what the word is. These activities represent major building blocks for reading.

If your child shows an early interest in wanting to read, encourage it. Help develop a basic vocabulary, recognizable by both sound and sight. Show how words fit together to make simple statements.

Continue to read to your child on a regular basis. This will help maintain a high level of interest. Ask questions about what you have read. Factual questions develop memory skills, and questions that begin with "Why . . ." or "What would have happened if . . ." teach critical thinking.

Enjoy words with your child. Have fun with language. Appreciate the marvel of this wonderful gift by using the tools of the written and spoken word to bring glory to God through the sharing of ideas.

chapter 42

Anger Management for Kids

Bradley walked into the house, slamming the door shut. He threw his jacket and books on the floor. Then he looked in the refrigerator and complained that there was never anything to eat. He went into the family room and turned on the TV. His mother told him he couldn't watch television until his homework was done. He blew up and was sent to his room. There he slammed the door and began to throw stuff around. Bradley was angry. And everyone in the house knew it.

Some children may be so prone to outbursts of anger that parents are afraid to correct their child for fear it will trigger another conflict. Some parents are actually intimidated and manipulated by their child's outbursts. Many wonder, what can I do to help my child manage anger?

First, know that everyone becomes angry; anger is a human emotion. So anger is not in itself a sin. What the anger is about (Does it agree with God's anger?) and what an individual does with the anger, on the other hand, may well become sinful.

Anger management follows God's plan for Christian living. The Bible says, "Everyone should be quick to listen, slow to speak and slow to become angry, for man's anger does not bring about the righteous life that God desires" (James 1:19,20). That's godly advice. In this biblical context, consider the following points as you teach your child how to manage anger.

- Begin with yourself. How does your child see you express anger? So much of what a child does is modeled after his or her parents. Can a parent expect a child to manage anger if the parent explodes in anger?

- Don't react to your child's anger with more emotion. That will only raise the tension level.

- If your child is totally out of control, send the child to his or her bedroom or some other quiet place. It is impossible to reason with someone who is out of control.

- After the emotion of the anger has worked its way out, help your child put the cause(s) for being angry into appropriate words.

- Realize that the event which started the outburst may not be the real source of anger. Is your child feeling insecure or unloved? Or is there a problem with a friend?

- After you have talked through an incident in a non-angry manner, help your child develop an action-oriented plan to correct the situation.

- Finally, look for times when your child has shown an appropriate response to a situation and compliment such positive behavior when it occurs. More is accomplished by praising good behavior than by criticizing bad behavior.

Every child needs to learn that there are appropriate ways to deal with anger. Parents always need to be teaching the basics of anger management. And all Christian parents need to set the godly example that David expressed when he wrote, "In your anger do not sin" (Psalm 4:4).

chapter 43

Christian Fatherhood

Any man can become a father. But it takes effort and prayer to be a successful Christian dad. But we have help. God's Word provides all the necessary instructions.

The first step to success is not even related to parenting skills. Rather, it comes from a Christian husband's wanting to love and serve his wife. Paul wrote, "Husbands ought to love their wives as their own bodies" (Ephesians 5:28). Children develop a feeling of security when they see their father showing love for their mother. At the same time, they are learning the marks of a healthy marital relationship.

Some fathers are not always able to be with their families on a regular basis. Their children may not always have good opportunities to witness a healthy marriage bond between their father and mother. Those fathers must also make every effort to teach their children to love and respect their mother. A successful dad is always building up and reinforcing the mother's role to the child.

A successful dad also prays for and with his children. He prays for the Holy Spirit to work and keep faith in his children's hearts. He prays for himself, asking for the wisdom to know how to handle their difficulties. He prays for their health and safety. He prays that his children will select good friends, do well in school, and eventually find godly spouses.

A successful dad loves his children. He is actually able to tell them of his love. Just as Jesus "took the children in his arms" (Mark 10:16), a dad will show physical signs of love. Even as children get older, they continue to need to hear of their dad's love for them. They need to feel it as well through hugs. Knowing and feeling their father's love provides children with a strong sense of security.

A successful dad teaches. Certainly he teaches about God's love and how to pray. But he also teaches letters, numbers, and colors. He may also teach how to dribble a basketball, ride a bike, and have fun. A successful father is also always interested in the accomplishments of his children. He is more ready to praise and compliment than to criticize. A godly dad also knows that he teaches a lot of lessons by his example.

A successful dad gives of his time to his children. He will read to them, listen to their dreams, and go to their events. He finds joy in being with all the members of his family.

A successful dad will also listen to his children. He may not always agree with what he hears, but he wants them to know that their opinions are valued. He will spend more time listening than talking.

A successful dad will also discipline his children. He teaches them the difference between right and wrong and tells them that doing right is a way of showing love for Jesus.

A successful dad is not measured by the amount of money he spends on his children but, rather, by what he does to lead his children to Jesus.

chapter 44

Bedtime Habits

For many parents and children, bedtime becomes a conflict of wills. Challenges like "I don't want to go to bed yet," "Do I have to go to bed already?" and "Why can't I stay up a little longer?" are common. So how much sleep do children really need?

Generally, elementary-school-aged children need at least nine hours of sleep. Preschoolers need ten or more. More is always better. Children deprived of normal sleep for even one night will frequently become irritable and tired. Children deprived of normal sleep for several nights will show personality changes and learn more slowly.

Getting children into bed and then getting them to stay in bed can be a daunting chore. For families that struggle with a bedtime ordeal, the following suggestions may be helpful:

- Have the same bedtime routine at the same time every night. If children are permitted to stay up later on the weekend, it should not be more than an hour later. Any more than that throws off the body's natural sleep-awake pattern.

- Try to limit physical activities, caffeinated soft drinks, scary movies, or computer games right before the bedtime routine begins. They tend to be stimulating.

- ✝ A structured order for putting on pj's, having an evening snack, story time, and prayer time will create a comforting atmosphere of routine and predictability. Try to keep each activity within a consistent time frame night after night.

- ✝ This is an excellent time to read a Bible story, sing a hymn, make up special prayers, and perhaps review memory work.

- ✝ After the routine is over, tuck your child into bed—that gives a feeling of security. Give a final kiss, turn off the lights (except for perhaps a night-light), and leave the room.

- ✝ If your child comes out of the bedroom, he or she needs to be walked back into the room and put into bed again. This is not the time for one more story or an "I forgot to tell you . . ."

- ✝ If your child is very upset and can't relax, a brief back massage and soft words of assurance may be quite helpful. Soft relaxing music may also be comforting.

- ✝ If your child becomes quite emotional, do not lie down with her or him. Lying down to calm your child will only reinforce the acting-out behavior. To calm a troubled child, sit on a chair in the room, but do not engage in conversation.

An evening that ends in calmness and structure, centered on prayer, brings about a restful night's sleep. "I will lie down and sleep in peace, for you alone, O Lord, make me dwell in safety" (Psalm 4:8).

chapter 45

Divorce and Kids

Divorce hurts kids! About 60 percent of all children living today in America will spend part of their childhoods in single-parent families. That's a lot of kids being affected by divorce.

Divorce also occurs in Christian families. That is not what God intended. God planned for a husband and wife to live together and raise their children. Sin has weakened the family structure. But the simple truth is this: God loves both those children and the adults affected by divorce. And he promises to help them. "I am the LORD, your God, who takes hold of your right hand and says to you, Do not fear; I will help you" (Isaiah 41:13).

Often divorcing parents will say the divorce is really in the best interests of the children. That's rarely true. It is a statement more often intended to soothe a guilty conscience. As a child psychologist, I frequently become involved in child custody disputes. I truly believe that if parents were aware of how much divorce hurts children, they would be more willing to try to resolve their differences and remain steadfast in their marriage commitment to each other.

One of the major effects of divorce is that it produces a lot of change. There may be a change in housing, neighborhood, school, and certainly financial resources. There may be a change in daily routines, responsibilities, discipline, and time spent with each parent. There is even change in relationships. Changes bring anxiety for both adults and children.

If you find yourself in the role of the divorced single parent, consider the following suggestions:

- Stay connected to God and his Word. He will lead you through this difficult time.
- Develop a Christian support system. Consider developing a support network in your church.
- Continue to assure your children of your love for them. Remind them that the divorce is not their fault.
- Realize that with the divorce, your children now live in two families. Each family has a way of doing things.
- Continue to tell your children that God (and you) expect them to love and respect the other parent.
- Try to keep things in your children's lives consistent.
- Do not talk to your children about adult issues such as missed support checks, court dates, or past problems. You will want to make a clear confession regarding right and wrong in God's eyes. At the same time be careful that you don't "bad mouth" the other parent.
- Do not use your children as pawns in arguments.
- Don't make your children feel guilty for having fun when spending time with the other parent.
- Do not involve a "new friend" in the lives of your children unless this will be a lasting relationship.

The less conflict there is between divorcing parents, the easier it will be for children to adjust. And remember, no matter what the trials of single parenthood may be, God is there to hold you and your children in his hand.

chapter 46

Challenges That Come with Change

God does not change. His love and his promise of help is always there. We can always depend on that. God's promise "Surely I am with you always, to the very end of the age" (Matthew 28:20) assumes that there will be changes, not only in our individual lives but throughout the ages.

So life is full of changes, and the uncertainty of change is hard on both children and adults. We like predictability and stability. They lead to feelings of comfort and security. Change creates an unsettled feeling. Change upsets regular routines and feelings of peace. Change often brings us to the brink of the unknown. This, in turn, can lead us to wish that things would somehow revert back to the way they were.

The death of a friend or relative, the divorce of parents, or the serious illness of a parent will bring major changes to a family. These changes will affect daily life. A parent's new job, a move to a different home, a change of school, or a friend's moving away can all produce some discomfort. Even seemingly small changes, like changing seats in school, getting a different babysitter, or changing a bedtime routine may produce feelings of unease.

All change is accompanied by emotions. These may include sadness, anger, and worry.

Adults often have an easier time dealing with change than children. Adults have experienced many changes. Sometimes they're the cause of the change. Adults are able to see how God has helped them work through changes in the past. Perhaps they can see the benefits of past changes and the blessings in upcoming changes. Children do not necessarily have that level of maturity or understanding.

When changes occur, consider doing the following:

- Prepare your child for any anticipated changes. Knowing about a change in advance is helpful.

- Explain the reasons for a change to your child. But remember, this does not necessarily remove the emotional pain.

- Listen to your child's hurts. Do not downplay feelings or dismiss emotions.

- Be positive about change. Explain that even changes that are painful or challenging also offer new opportunities for growing.

- Include your child in plans that lead to change. Help your child understand that God gives us the power to cause some changes in our lives.

- Teach your child about things that never change: God's love, his forgiveness, his promise to be with you and bless you, and your future eternal life with him in heaven.

- Finally, pray about the change. Ask God to help everyone make the adjustment.

chapter 47

Sex and Gender Education

Gary and Marge have always said they're going to talk to their children about sex. Neither of their parents had ever talked with them about sex, and now they recall how unprepared they felt about their own sexual development. Some of their learning was gained from dirty jokes and stories from friends. Much of their information centered on sexual activity. They are determined to do a better job; they just don't know when. And they keep putting it off.

One Sunday afternoon as the family is home together, four-year-old Vicki asks, "Can I be pregnant?" Later seven-year-old Amy asks when she can wear a bra. Still later Dad finds 10-year-old Brian and 12-year-old Kevin looking and giggling at the ladies' underwear ads in the newspaper.

Marge answered Vicki with a simple no. She told Amy, "Don't worry about a bra yet." Gary scolded the boys for having filthy minds. Missed opportunities!

Sex and gender talk should not be a one-time conversation. Nor should it be a "I did the talk, and now it's over." Sex education is an ongoing conversation between parents and children that centers on the Bible text that says, "I am fearfully and wonderfully made" (Psalm 139:14).

A lot of parents want to teach their children about sex, but the right time never seems to occur. They may feel awkward about talking to their children about sexual development because they have not talked about sexual matters with each other. Often the topic of sex is associated with uncomfortable feelings.

Parents need to look for teachable moments. Vicki's question indicates that she wants to know what being pregnant means. Amy is curious about the when and the how of her own physical development. The boys want to know what female bodies are like. Parents need to seize these opportunities to provide sexual information in a positive way.

Many parents feel that their only responsibility is to tell their children to come to them with any questions they might have about sex. When their children don't come with questions, the parents are relieved, believing the issues have worked themselves out. In truth, unless the topic of sex has been openly discussed by parents, it's unlikely that children will come with questions. They may go to friends, look in magazines, or go on the Internet.

It's appropriate for Christian parents to emphasize that sex and gender are gifts from God. They need to stress that, as a gift, the act of sexual intercourse is meant to be enjoyed between a man and a woman in marriage. The details of this topic should never be approached as a list of bad things. God created Adam and Eve as male and female before sin entered the picture. And parents should view their intimate lives—the way they are loving and considerate, caring and concerned for one another's well-being—as working models for their children to observe.

Children are going to be curious about sex. That's good. But they're ready to learn at different levels. A three-year-old needs to know the basic difference between boys and girls. Picture books showing the physical differences can help. This is also the time to talk about good and bad touching.

Children in the middle years (4 to 9) need to begin to know some of the basics of sexual biology and reproduction. At this age it's appropriate to refer to body parts by their correct names. But don't overload children of this age with too much information, and don't introduce new topics that will make them feel uncomfortable.

During the preteen and early teen years (10 to 14), children really need a lot of information. They need to learn the physical changes related to puberty. This is also a time to talk about homosexuality and appropriate and inappropriate sexual activity. There needs to be a talk about sexual activity between husband and wife and the processes of conception and childbirth. Again, don't overwhelm your children with too much information. At the same time, be proactive; don't wait for them to get their sexual information from the school locker room.

Some parents worry that if they talk to their children about sex, their children will become sexually active. That really is not true. One of the challenges is to find a balance between too much information and no information.

Books on the subject of sex education, written from a Christian perspective, can be especially helpful. Look for materials that include diagrams and provide good ways to begin a conversation on a variety of sex- and gender-related topics.

This is an ongoing process that will change as children get older. Parents need to continually look for those teachable moments to review and broaden their children's understanding of sex and gender.

chapter 48

Teaching Kindness

It's almost the last thing we hear as we leave the worship service in church each week. The pastor instructs the people to "live in harmony with one another." It's an exhortation rooted in the last verse of Ephesians chapter 4, in which Saint Paul tells us to "Be kind and compassionate to one another."

Kindness, compassion, and harmony do not seem to be a good fit in a society that places so much value on competition, assertiveness, and personal victory. Children do not automatically learn to be kind as they grow up. Nor is it their natural inclination. Children must be taught to be kind and compassionate.

Your children will learn kindness and compassion as you teach them about Jesus. Every Bible lesson has a central truth about God's love for all mankind. Point to how Jesus demonstrated kindness and compassion in everything he did.

Children will also learn these characteristics as they see parents living in harmony with each other. They will adopt harmony as a personal value and make it an important part of their lives. As children see parents doing acts of kindness for others, they see the value of compassion. To teach kindness to your child, you will need to model it in your own life.

We can also teach our children how to show kindness by placing them into situations that will give them opportunities to demonstrate kindness to other people.

Using "please" and "thank you" as part of their vocabulary, befriending a hurt child or a defenseless classmate, or doing helpful things around the house are all acts of kindness. Kindness is also reinforced when parents teach their children to pray for others who are in need or trouble.

Children can also learn kindness and compassion by becoming involved in various volunteer activities. Your family can be part of a cleaning crew at church. Children may help buy food for a local food pantry. They can help an elderly neighbor transport groceries, cut the lawn, or wash the windows.

Parents need to let their children know how much their acts of kindness are appreciated. Compliments cost us nothing, and yet they are worth so much to the one who is waiting to hear that a job was done well.

The real secret is to continue to grow in your own capacity to be kind and compassionate to others. The motivation for living in harmony with others—for being kind and compassionate—is that these acts are ways of showing love for Jesus.

When you practice the skills and attitudes that are associated with kindness and compassion, you may not be giving your child a competitive edge in society, but it will demonstrate the love for the Lord Jesus that is in their hearts.

chapter 49

A Checklist for Christian Parents

Does either of the following expressions describe your approach to teaching your children? "Do as I say, not as I do." Or, "Monkey see, monkey do."

Neither is totally effective. A better saying would be—"Learn from what I teach you, and watch what I do."

Children learn best when words of instruction are reinforced by the examples they see. They become confused when what they observe in your behavior is different from your words. So, what are your children hearing in your words; and what are they seeing in your behavior?

Yes **No** Do your children hear you talk about your love for Jesus?

Yes **No** Do they see you pray and read the Bible?

Yes **No** Do they hear you talk about God's blessings to the family?

Yes **No** Do they see an accepting, thankful attitude?

Yes **No** Are they taught why going to church is important?

Yes **No** Do they observe you taking an active part in worship?

Yes **No** Do they hear you singing?

Yes	**No**	Do you teach them to bring an offering to God?
Yes	**No**	Do they see you setting aside money for an offering?
Yes	**No**	Do you instruct your children to be kind and caring to all people?
Yes	**No**	Do they see you showing respect for everyone?
Yes	**No**	Do your children observe love being exchanged between parents?
Yes	**No**	Are your children taught the value of work?
Yes	**No**	Do they see you doing things to help others?
Yes	**No**	Can they observe you supporting the members of your own family?
Yes	**No**	Are they taught to take responsibility for their actions?
Yes	**No**	Have they seen you admit to, and apologize for, a wrong word or action?
Yes	**No**	Are they taught to be polite?
Yes	**No**	Do they hear you say please and thank you, I'm sorry, or I forgive you?
Yes	**No**	Do you teach your children to talk about their anger, frustration, or disappointment?
Yes	**No**	Do your children see you in control of your actions and emotions?
Yes	**No**	Do you teach your children that losing one's temper never solves a problem?

Yes **No** Do you teach your children that we are to show love for God daily?

Yes **No** Are your children given words of encouragement for the positive things they do?

Yes **No** Do they learn that God is in control and that he will bring good out of difficulty?

Yes **No** Do they see an accepting attitude, without bitterness, when times are difficult?

Children learn from what they hear and see. It is important for them to observe the behaviors their parents are teaching to reinforce the things you have taught them. Make sure that all of your actions agree with your words.